KTG know the game

Gymnastics

Brian Stocks and Eddie Arnold

A & C Black (Publishers) Ltd
35 Bedford Row, London WC1R 4JH

CW00327701

Contents

Introduction

The dominance in women's gymnastics of Russia and Romania, and the emergence of China in men's gymnastics to challenge the battles of Japan and Russia, have recently brought the electricity of the sport of gymnastics to a new generation. The sport has become one of the largest participation sports in Great Britain, being on nearly every school curriculum for both boys and girls.

This book is offered to the coach, teacher and young gymnast as a means of gaining a practical understanding of gymnastics at its most basic level. At this level the book is intended for both boys and girls, as little distinction is made between the sexes during their first steps in gymnastics. The gymnast has usually been referred to as 'he', but this should be taken to mean 'he or she' where appropriate.

The book includes many of the movements which appear in the British Amateur Gymnastics Association Coca Cola Award Scheme. In fact, the interest generated by this scheme suggests that gymnastics is now the 'in' sport and will

continue to be so for a long time to come: well over five million badges have been awarded so far.

One word of caution: safety is a vital part of the practice of gymnastics and considerations of safety must always be borne in mind. *It is essential that all gymnasts and coaches read the section on safety (p. 39) before starting to perform any gymnastics.*

Acknowledgements

Line drawings by Bob Currier
All black and white photographs by Eileen Langsley/Supersport
(inside front cover—Oksana Omelianchik, USSR, straddled splits handstand balance)
Front cover photograph by Sporting Pictures (Heather Carter, USA, straddled planché on beam)

2

Ecaterina Szabo, Romania, 'Y' scale balance

Preparatory skills

1 Forward roll

This is the first and most basic movement, which must be learned by any beginner gymnast.

Start from a squat position, placing the hands, about shoulder width apart, on the floor in front of you. The legs are then straightened while *the chin is placed on the chest*. This ensures that the hips are raised high enough and the back is rounded to allow the rolling movement to take place. The arms are then bent as you place your neck on the floor. Bending the arms causes the gymnast to become off-balance and the rolling motion automatically takes place. Aim to keep your legs straight as the forward roll commences.

In the last phase of the roll, bend your legs tightly so that your feet are placed on the floor close to your hips. As the feet make contact with the floor, shift your head, chest and arms forward so as to get your body weight over your feet.

Note: the forward roll should be done without using your hands to stand up from the floor. Very young or small children find attempting the whole movement very difficult for this reason. Outlined below is a method attempting the movement in parts.

Lying on your back, draw the knees up to the chest and rock backwards and forwards. Whilst rocking, alternately stretch and bend the legs to make the movement more powerful and reach forward with the arms as the bottom and feet touch the ground. This method will allow the performer to stand up without the assistance of the hands on the ground.

Standing with the legs apart, put your hands and head between your legs until the back of your neck touches the ground; push off the legs and roll onto the back.

2 Handstand with support (partner)

The handstand is one of *the fundamental positions* in gymnastics and must therefore be really well learned.

Start from a standing position with arms raised overhead – *stretch*. Then take a long step forward, bending the front leg, and place both hands on the floor, approximately *shoulder width apart*. The

fingers should point forward. At this point, straighten the front leg while at the same time kicking the back leg up into the handstand position.

During the movement into handstand, the shoulders must move forward over the hands and then return to a position directly over the hands once the handstand position has been attained. This feeling of balance is something the gymnast must learn, as it is essential for the learning of more advanced movements later on. It is recommended, therefore, that this movement should be practised for at least ten minutes every day.

The handstand itself must be *straight*. The partner must help in adjusting the balance and helping the gymnast to achieve the correct position. To develop the straight position, learn to press the legs rigidly together, concentrating on holding the stomach in and tightening the buttocks. Once the straight position has

been attained, the partner can now aid the gymnast further by momentarily releasing him, so that the gymnast can get used to adjusting his own balance.

Remember, the gymnast must do most of the work – he must not be over-supported. Be careful to make sure that the gymnast is in a vertical position; holding the gymnast at an angle means that he is not learning how to hold a handstand.

3 Backward roll

Start from a squat position, with back well rounded. Allow your body weight to fall back over the heels until your bottom makes contact with the floor. The hands are then moved quickly to a position just above the shoulders, with the fingers facing the body, the palms away from the body and the elbows held high, as the rolling movement takes place. Place your chin on your chest so that as little weight as possible is put on your head during the backward roll. (See top p.5.)

As soon as the shoulders make contact with the floor, push the floor away by straightening your arms. This arm push raises the hips so that the movement may be finished in a squat standing position.

The backward roll may be supported by taking hold of the gymnast's waist as he rolls onto his shoulder. The spotter can then lift the gymnast's hips over his head to aid the actual rolling movement, while at the same time reducing the amount of weight felt by the gymnast on his head.

4 Front support jump to crouch

The front support position must be held with the body straight and the hands placed directly below the shoulders. To hold this straight body position, clench the buttocks tightly and hold the stomach in.

From this position, hollow your back (i.e. moving the stomach closer to the floor) and then quickly raise your hips by pushing with your feet. At the same time your shoulders will automatically move forward over your hands, allowing you to arrive easily in the crouch position.

5 Headstand with knees bent

Start from a crouch position and then place the hands and forehead on the floor to form a triangle (as shown) with the head approximately thirty centimetres in front of the hands. The arms will then be bent to an angle of roughly 90°.

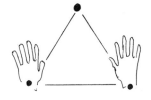

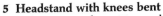

Slowly move the feet in closer to your hands until the hips lie directly above this triangular base. Push down with the hands until the feet leave the floor and 'feel' for the balance position. The knees should be bent tightly, with the back held straight. This straight back position

5

allows the gymnast's weight to be evenly distributed over his hands and head. Hollowing the back tends to put excessive pressure on the gymnast's head and neck.

The headstand can be supported by quite simply taking hold of the gymnast's hips, and making sure that he adopts the correct position.

Note: it is most important that the gymnast balances on his *forehead* and not any other part of his head.

6 Bridge
Start from lying on your back with your knees bent (so that your feet are close to your bottom) and your hands flat on the floor close to your head. From this position, push against the floor with hands and feet to arrive in a bridge. The movement is completed when both the arms and legs are completely straight. Make sure that your ankles and knees are pressed tightly together.

The ideal bridge position is one where the shoulders lie directly over the hands.

It may be necessary at first to assist the beginner, as this position is not easy to attain until the required flexibility in shoulders and spine has been developed. Support can be given by lifting the gymnast under his shoulders as he tries to

adopt the bridge position. At the very beginning, it is easier for the gymnast to hold on to the spotter's ankles as he is

being supported, but this should be dispensed with as soon as possible.

7 Squat onto and jump off box with straight body
This movement starts with a short run and small hop (hurdle step) to land with two feet in front of the box. Place your hands on the box top and jump hard from the floor, concentrating on raising the hips as much as possible. In order to raise the hips effectively it is important to press hard with the hands against the box, allowing the shoulders to move forward slightly over the hands. This arm and shoulder movement also allows the gymnast to bring his feet close to his hands to arrive in squat position on the box.

In jumping off the box, quickly straighten your legs and *stretch* for the ceiling (from fingers to toes). Keep your head up in the jump, just focussing at the

spot on the floor where you intend to land. Try *not* deliberately to look downwards. On landing, bend at the ankles, knees, and hips to cushion the landing and quickly come to attention. it is important to work at landing in a still position, without any extra movement of the feet. The landing from any gymnastic movement is a very important factor, and is something into which even top-class gymnasts put a lot of concentration.

It may be necessary to assist the gymnast in either one or both phases of this movement. In the first phase support can be given from the side, by taking hold of the gymnast under his near shoulder and stomach. In the jump-off phase, the spotter should stand either to one side or in front of the gymnast and take hold of his chest, making sure that he does not rotate when coming in to land.

(For further work with the box, see the section on apparatus, p.27.)

8 Astride jump from box (sometimes called a star jump or stretched straddle jump)

This jump is in many ways similar to the one previously described.

In jumping from the box top, bend and then quickly straighten your legs. *Stretch* for the ceiling, keeping your head up while just focussing on a spot on the floor where you intend to land. As you leave

the box top, spread your legs and arms as much as possible so that your body forms a star shape in the air. Then on approaching the floor, quickly bring your legs together and attempt to land still, without any extra movement of the feet.

To help support this movement, a spotter can again stand to the side and support the gymnast under his chest to make sure he does not over-rotate.

9 Leapfrog over partner

This movement starts with a short run and small hurdle step to land with two feet in front of the partner. Place your hands on your partner's back and jump from the floor while at the same time pressing hard against your partner's back. It is important for the gymnast to raise both the hips and the chest (keeping the head up) so that he will be able to vault over his partner.

As you press down on your partner's back, straddle your legs wide, so as to avoid touching him with your legs. Try to land in a still position. A spotter can again be present to help out in the way previously described.

Note: it is important for the partner to form a solid platform over which the gymnast can vault. He should bend forward to approximately 90° (between legs and trunk), with feet spread apart and hands resting firmly on his legs, just above the knees.

10 Standing upward jump with half turn

Bend your legs slightly and then quickly

7

jump upwards, throwing the arms upwards as the feet leave the floor.

To create the half turn the gymnast must move his head and arms in the direction of the intended turn as he leaves the floor. If he wishes to turn to his left, he should *look* over his left shoulder, while at the same time raising his arms overhead in such a way that the right arm moves towards the left side of his body. The right arm should pass in front of the gymnast's head and the arms must then stay close to one another as the turn is completed.

Try to land in a still position with arms raised overhead.

Arabesque on beam

Basic skills

1 From astride sitting, circle roll sideways to face opposite direction

For the purpose of discussion we will assume the gymnast intends to turn to his left.

1. *View from above*

Keeping your arms by your sides, lean to the left so that the left elbow first makes contact with the floor. This should then be immediately followed by the left side of your body and the left shoulder. On reaching the left shoulder, concentrate on rolling along the upper back from the left shoulder to the right shoulder.

When the right shoulder contacts the floor, roll down the right side of your body until the right elbow touches the floor, and then return into an astride sitting position.

At this point, the gymnast should be facing in the opposite direction. At all points through the roll, the gymnast should be bent at the waist with his legs straddled, i.e. the same body position should be maintained throughout the movement.

It may be necessary at first for the coach to assist the gymnast through this movement, as many beginners become disorientated when first trying it.

1. *View from the side*

2 Headstand with legs straight

This movement is approached in exactly the same way as the headstand with knees bent.

Once in the bent leg headstand position, slowly straighten your legs to the ceiling, making sure that your back is *straight* at all times. The back is kept straight by clenching the muscles of the buttocks tightly and holding the stomach in.

The headstand can also be approached by raising into it with straight legs from a crouch position. This is a slightly more difficult version, but the technique is still very much the same as that previously described.

A spotter can help the gymnast by taking hold of his hips and making sure that he adopts the correct body position.

3 Backward roll to astride

This movement is started in exactly the same way as described earlier for the backward roll, and in many ways the technique used is basically the same.

As you roll over your back onto your shoulders and neck, begin to straighten your legs. Then, as soon as your hands are placed firmly on the floor, push hard so as to raise your hips as much as possible. With the hips well raised, it is possible to keep the legs completely straight throughout the latter phase of the movement.

When your hips are directly over your hands, straddle the legs and lower the feet to the floor close to your hands to finish in astride stand. To make sure you

actually finish in astride stand, it is necessary to push the floor with both hands, so that your head and chest can be raised above your hips.

A spotter can help the gymnast in the final phase of this movement by supporting his hips as he lowers his legs to the floor.

4 Cartwheel

This is a movement that passes through a side handstand position (with legs straddled). To start this movement you can either face the direction in which you intend to go, or stand sideways on. The first method is recommended here.

Raise your arms and place your leading leg forward on the floor. From this position bend the front leg and your waist and place your first hand on the floor. If you lead with your left leg, then it is the left hand which is first placed on the floor.

Once the first hand makes contact with the floor, straighten your front leg, while *at the same time* kicking upwards with your back leg. The movement continues by rocking over onto the second hand while passing through a side handstand position. As you move over your second hand, push strongly against the floor so as to rock over onto your second leg and then into a stretched position with arms raised overhead. Starting with the left leg the sequence of movements is left foot, left hand, right hand, right foot.

Try to do the complete movement along a straight line, emphasising the point of pushing strongly with your second hand so as to arrive in a stretched standing position.

To assist the gymnast in performing

this movement a spotter should stand to the back of him as he performs the cartwheel. If the gymnast leads with his left leg the spotter should place his right hand on the gymnast's left hip (i.e. hands crossed); left arm over right arm. The spotter is then able to help the gymnast move through the side handstand, as well as aiding his overall rotation.

5 Handstand

This is a natural progression from the handstand with support as described earlier. The handstand should be held with body straight, emphasising complete extension in the shoulders. To do this, try pressing the toes towards the ceiling. It is important to avoid letting the body weight just rest on the hands; concentrate on pressing the body up as far as possible.

The next stage in learning the handstand is to practise it against a wall. Before attempting this, the gymnast must be able to support his body weight on straight arms.

First of all, place your hands roughly thirty centimetres (twelve inches) from the wall and then kick up into handstand. Learn both to kick to handstand and

return to floor (by pressing away from the wall) without collapsing. Once you can do this confidently, gradually approach the handstand by moving your hands closer and closer to the wall (until your fingers are only an inch or two away) so that you are forced into learning a *straight* handstand. You should then start practising moving your feet away from the wall – without coming down to the floor – to hold the handstand free, and then returning to the wall again.

Balance can be maintained by pressing the fingers strongly into the floor. This is particularly important when you feel you are about to overbalance.

Eventually you should start practising the handstand in the middle of the gym floor, learning to kick into a held handstand. The movement will have been thoroughly learned when you can do this without any bending of the arms or walking on the hands to regain balance.

6 Forward roll to standing position

Start the movement from a squat position as already described. As you roll over towards your lower back, quickly bend your knees and place your feet on the floor as close to the hips as possible. As soon as the feet contact the floor, shift

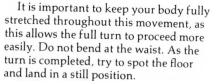

your head, chest and arms forward so as to get your body weight over the feet. Then immediately stand up, with arms raised overhead.

If necessary, a spotter can stand in front of the gymnast and take hold of his arms to help him get his weight over his feet.

7 Standing upward jump with full turn
This movement is basically a natural progression of the jump with half turn described earlier. As you bend your legs,

swing your arms backward in preparation for the upward jump. The arms must then swing forwards and upwards as the legs are straightened when actually performing the jump.

If you are going to turn to your left, *the right arm must move across the front of your body* (in front of your head) towards the left arm, as your feet leave the floor. At the same time, look over your left shoulder, and try to keep the arms as close together as possible throughout the turn.

It is important to keep your body fully stretched throughout this movement, as this allows the full turn to proceed more easily. Do not bend at the waist. As the turn is completed, try to spot the floor and land in a still position.

Make sure you first try the movement on soft mats, so that if balance is lost, you are in a position to land safely. This movement can also be practised quite safely on a trampoline, as this allows the gymnast more time in which to complete the turn.

8 Diagonal vault, one leg take-off
This movement begins with a short run up, at an angle of approximately 45°, to a vaulting box set sideways on.

If you intend to take off from your right leg, you must run at the box from the left-hand side (as you face it). As you place your right foot on the floor in

preparation for the vault itself, place your left hand on the box top while at the same time swinging the left leg in a forward and upward direction. Be sure not to take off too close to the box as you could well kick it with your swinging leg.

As soon as you take off from the floor, press down hard with the left hand, to help you pass over the box top. Once the right leg (take-off leg) starts to move over the box, you must place your right hand on the box top and continue pressing, while releasing the left hand so as to allow your body to land on the other side. The legs should be brought together as they pass over the box top.

A spotter can help the gymnast by standing on the other side of the box and to his rear as he passes over the box. He then simply supports the gymnast's waist as he performs the vault.

9 Tucked jump upward from box top

Bend your legs and swing your arms back. Then quickly straighten your legs while at the same time swinging your arms forward and upwards. This is important to get maximum height in the jump. Try and stretch as much as possible going into the jump, while keeping the head up, just focussing on the spot on the floor where you intend to land.

At the height of the jump, quickly bend your legs and bring your knees up to your chest, and then just as quickly stretch out again in preparation for the landing.

A spotter should stand in front of, or slightly to one side of, the gymnast and take hold of his chest to make sure he does not over-rotate.

10 Straddle vault over buck or box broadways

Start from a short run and small hurdle step, landing on two feet in front of the box.

Jump upwards and quickly place the hands on the box top. At this point it is important to push strongly against the box so as to allow the hips to rise to at least shoulder level. As the hips rise,

straddle your legs as wide as possible and allow the shoulders to move slightly forward over the hands. Once in flight, bring your feet together while at the same time quickly stretching your body in preparation for the landing. *Concentrate on keeping your head and chest up.* If the push has been strong enough, then it will carry the gymnast up and over the box. Problems occur with gymnasts who do not push hard enough or long enough.

A useful practice at the beginning is to straddle *onto* the box, and then jump off. This helps the gymnast to appreciate how wide he has to straddle his legs in order to achieve the movement, and also how high he has to raise his hips in the process.

A spotter should stand in front of the gymnast to support his chest, in case the gymnast catches his feet (a common

mistake) and pitches head first onto the floor. In the early stages, it is advisable to place a soft crash mat on the other side of the box, for the landing.

Hyperflexed standing scale or 'wine glass'

Progressive skills

1 Handstand, forward roll

Kick into handstand, adopting a straight body position. It is preferable to hold the handstand for at least a second to show you have control over the position.

In handstand, stretch out in the shoulders and allow the feet to move forward over the hands. Once balance is lost and you can feel the sensation of falling forward, try to look at the spot on the floor with which your shoulders will make contact. Then at the last moment, duck your head under, placing the chin on the chest, so as to allow the neck and shoulders to make the first contact with the floor. As soon as the shoulders touch the floor, round your back and proceed into the forward roll, which is exactly the same as that previously described.

In the fall forward from handstand, there will first of all be a natural tendency to bend the arms. This is quite acceptable, but later on, as you become more competent, try to keep the arms straight. Although more advanced, the straight arm roll is not particularly difficult to learn and can be picked up quite quickly by most beginners.

2 Forward roll with straight legs to straddle

Start the forward roll in the same way as the ordinary roll. While rolling over your back, the legs must be straight. As you approach the lower part of your back in the roll, straddle the legs *wide* – the wider the straddle, the easier the movement is to perform.

15

As the heels approach the floor, place the hands on the floor in between the legs and close to the crutch. Once the heels touch the floor, push hard with the hands and lean well forward, trying to get the head and chest forward of the feet. It is important to continue pressing the floor for the maximum amount of time, that is, until the fingers leave the floor. Do not try to stand up too soon, keep the body bent forward until your body weight is completely over the feet. Only then should you stretch out in the straddle stand position.

A more advanced version is to do this movement without using the hands. This, however, depends on your ability to straddle the legs wide and bend well forward at the waist.

A spotter can aid the gymnast by standing behind him and pushing his hips forward until he is in the straddle stand position.

3 Backward roll passing through handstand

Start in exactly the same way as for an ordinary backward roll. It is now important to make the hand movement to the shoulders *very fast*. As soon as the hands contact the floor, push hard while at the same time extending the hips and

legs to the ceiling. Again, hold your head in (chin on chest). Timing is important – the hip extension and arm push should take place at the same time.

This movement can be learned progressively by practising ordinary backward rolls while concentrating on pushing the hips to the ceiling without stretching out the legs. As you learn how to push into a straight arm position with hips directly overhead, then you can start to stretch out your legs. Little by little, the movement is built up in this fashion.

A spotter can help the gymnast by taking hold of his feet as his hands contact the floor and lifting him through to a straight handstand.

Ideally, this movement should be done to a held handstand.

4 Two cartwheels

Each cartwheel is exactly the same as that described earlier. However, the second cartwheel will always be done from a side-facing position.

On the first cartwheel, it is most important to push hard with the second hand that contacts the floor, as this is what initially creates the momentum for the second cartwheel. To allow the second cartwheel to proceed smoothly from the first, bend your legs slightly as the feet come into contact with the floor. If the legs are kept perfectly straight, then there will be a tendency to hesitate before moving into the second cartwheel. Concentrate hard on moving down a straight line.

When done correctly, you should have no problems doing a series of cartwheels in continuous fashion – making the series look like a wheel rolling down a mat.

5 High forward roll

This movement is basically a dive roll, in which there is a flight stage before going into the roll.

In the early stages, try this movement onto a couple of rolled-up mats (placed on top of one another) or onto a crash mat. A soft landing is necessary at this point.

First of all, attempt the dive roll from a standing position to land about one metre (three or four feet) from the take-off spot. This ensures that the roll will be completed. Keep your body bent in the dive and reach forward with outstretched arms for the floor. Your arms must contact the floor firmly and then immediately bend while you duck your head under and go into the roll. If you do not cushion the impact with your arms then too much weight will be felt on the back of your neck and back.

Later on, add a small run and try to dive further forward into the roll.

Ideally, as the gymnast becomes more advanced, the dive roll will be done from a strong run up and with straight body throughout.

6 Handstand, drop over to bridge

From the handstand position, stretch out in the shoulders and press the shoulders back so that they move behind the position of the hands. At the same time, allow the feet to move forward over the hands so that balance is lost. Arch the back strongly and maintain pressure with the hands, forcing the shoulders to stay behind the hands. This is important, as it helps you to avoid collapsing completely once the feet contact the floor. When the feet contact the floor, there will be a tendency to bend the legs and sag in the shoulders, which in turn causes the hips to drop. Hence, as soon as foot contact is made, immediately straighten your legs and press hard against the floor with your hands, so as to hold the bridge position with straight arms and legs.

The bridge itself is exactly the same as described earlier.

A spotter can assist the gymnast by supporting him under his near shoulder and lower back as he falls into the bridge position.

7 Headspring

Start from a squat position, placing both hands on the floor in front of you and immediately lowering your head to the floor (head slightly in front of your hands). At the same time straighten the

legs so that your feet leave the floor at about the same time as your forehead makes contact with the floor.

The legs continue forwards and upwards, first straightening, then extending the body. As the hips move forwards over your head, push strongly with your hands. You should continue to stretch out your body so that you adopt an arched position in flight, with arms held overhead. Maintain this completely stretched position until the feet make contact with the floor again.

A spotter can assist the gymnast by

placing one hand under his near shoulder and the other hand under his lower back.

8 Headspring from standing position on box

This is exactly the same movement as the headspring with the exception that in this case, the gymnast experiences a longer flight stage (from box top to floor). It is essential when learning this movement that a spotter be present to make sure that the gymnast does not over-rotate in the flight stage; also, the headspring should be done onto either a crash mat or a pile of very soft mats.

The arched position in flight is obviously maintained for a longer period of time, but as your feet and hips rotate under your shoulders, bring the head forward and try to spot the floor in preparation for the landing. It is important to sight the floor before landing, so as to prevent any possibility of jarring yourself.

9 Squat (through) vault

Start with a short run and small hurdle step to land with two feet in front of the box.

Jump towards the box and immediately place both hands on the box top (towards the far edge). The jump should be sufficiently powerful, coupled with the strong arm push to follow, to allow you to raise your hips to a level higher than your shoulders. As the hips rise, bend your legs and bring the knees to your chest while at the same time allowing your shoulders to travel forward over your hands. If the arm push has been strong enough, you will continue the flight over the box to land on the other side. Make sure to keep your head and chest up in the flight.

A spotter should be present to support the gymnast's chest in flight, just in case the gymnast catches his feet and nose-dives to the floor. In the early stages a crash mat should be placed on the far side of the box.

The spotting for this movement is the same as that for the headspring. The spotter should however be aware that the gymnast might extend his body too soon and come back on top of the box. Extra support must be given if this error is made.

10 Neckspring, box broadways

Approach this vault in the same way as mentioned for previous vaults. In many ways, this movement is similar to the headspring already described.

Place the hands centrally on the box top and jump, raising the hips well above shoulder level. As the hips rise, duck your head (chin on chest) and allow your arms to bend so as to place your neck and shoulders squarely on top of the box. At this point, the hips should still be slightly behind your hands, in the direction of travel, so that your knees lie roughly above your face. This part needs to be done quite quickly so as to prevent the hips from rocking too far forward too soon.

Allow the legs to swing in a forward and upward direction – that is, the body is straightened out. Then, as the hips pass in front of the hands, push strongly with the arms (until they are straight) while continuing to stretch out the body until it is *arched* in flight. It is important to continue pushing until the arms are perfectly straight – the fingers should be the last parts to leave the box. Maintain this extended body position until the feet contact the floor.

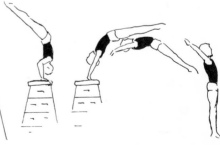

Advanced skills

1 Backflip

This movement is an essential basic to all advanced acrobatic skills, and it is therefore important that the gymnast develops a powerful backflip for the sake of future improvement.

From standing, sit back into an off-balance position while swinging the arms downwards. Do *not* lean forward over the feet as you sit back. At the lowest point in the sit, reverse the action and begin to extend your hips and legs (i.e. straighten out the body) in a backward and upward direction. Press back hard from the heels as you do this. During this second phase of the movement, the arms should be swinging forward, upward and overhead.

Move your head back as your arms move past it. In flight, the body must be arched with the shoulders completely extended.

The hands should contact the floor with the legs still behind them. From this bowed position, push hard from the floor while at the same time snapping the feet down to the ground. These two actions must occur simultaneously. Try to bounce out of the flip once the feet contact the floor again.

Physical support is very important in the early stages of learning a backflip, and so is the use of soft mats. The spotter should stand to one side, and hold the gymnast under his near thigh and lower back. Support should be given throughout the movement until the gymnast's hands contact the floor. Make sure the gymnast's hips do not drop in flight as this results in very heavy landing.

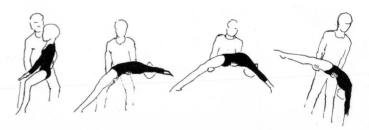

2 Round-off

This movement is developed from a cartwheel and is basically a cartwheel with one quarter turn. In the cartwheel, both hands and feet move along a straight line, but in the round-off, the second hand is placed slightly out of line with the first (see diagram below).

Start with a small run and skip step, stretching the arms overhead in the skip step. When leading with the left leg, the skip step consists of the following ground contacts – right foot, right foot, left foot, hand placement. *Lean well forward.* Bend the leading leg (say the left) and at the waist, to place the left hand on the floor. Immediately straighten the left leg while at the same time swinging the right leg upwards into the cartwheel action.

The body should twist around the left arm so as to place the right hand out of alignment with the left.

As soon as both hands are in contact with the floor, the legs should trail behind (in the direction of travel). Push hard and snap the legs down to the ground (while the quarter turn is completed).

You should land facing the direction from which you have come. Try to land with arms raised overhead and with the body as extended as possible.

3 Handstand through bridge and stand

This movement is a continuation of the handstand drop to bridge.

In this case, in the drop from handstand, try to get the feet as close to the hands as possible. Then, as soon as the feet contact the floor, keep your knees slightly bent and push hard from the floor with the hands, aiming to push the hips forward over your feet.

Any bending of the arms as the feet touch the floor will tend to destroy the movement. Try to keep your hips as high as possible at all times.

A spotter can assist the gymnast in a similar manner to that described for handstand through to bridge.

4 Handspring

The handspring starts in the same way as the round-off, with a run up and skip step, with the gymnast leaning well forward on the skip step.

It is important to take a long step into the handspring. Bend the leading leg, and attempt to place the hands as far forward as possible. There should be no obvious diving to the floor, as this destroys the movement to follow. Hence, try to stretch as much as possible in the shoulders. As the hands contact the floor, straighten the front leg while at the same time swinging the back leg upwards. These leg movements should be *very fast*.

Once the body weight is completely on the hands, push hard from the hands and shoulders, attempting to shrug your shoulders for even more lift. It is important to push hard from the floor with straight arms so as to prevent the shoulders from travelling forward over the hands. Any shoulder travel reduces the height of the final movement.

In flight, the body should be slightly arched with the arms held overhead. Try to land in an extended position, again with arms held overhead. The knees should bend only slightly on landing, with *no* bending at the waist.

The handspring is best learned from a raised platform with crash mats. The spotter supports the gymnast under the near shoulder and lower back and carries him through the entire movement. The degree of support is reduced as the gymnast improves.

At first try the handspring from stand,

kicking fast through handstand, before attempting the full movement. One or two spotters should be present to shape the movement.

5 Splits (forwards or sideways)

The forwards splits should be held with the knee facing up on the front leg and the knee facing down on the back leg – toes pointed. The body should be facing directly forward.

Ideally, the side splits should be held with knees facing up, but it is also quite acceptable if the knees face forwards. The trunk must be held upright with no

distinct arching of the lower back or forward lean.

In both types of splits, the arm should be held horizontally to the side.

In learning the splits, stand with the legs wide astride and place both hands on the floor between them. Gradually move the feet out wider until tension can be felt in the adductor muscles (on the upper part of the inside leg). Hold this position for about a minute each session. In time the full splits position will be reached.

Another exercise is to sit facing the wall bars with the legs straddled as wide as possible. Grasp the bars about chest height and try to pull the hips closer to the bars while allowing the legs to slide out. At the maximum point, hold the position from one to two minutes each session.

6 Cartwheel, one hand only

There is little difference between this movement and the ordinary cartwheel. The only real difference is that generally this movement must be done faster and with a more forceful push from the one arm support. As there is no rocking action over the hands, it is very important to push strongly from the floor so as to make sure you finish in a stretched standing position.

No matter which leg you lead with, either arm can be used for support, but it is recommended here that if, say, you lead with the left leg, then you would use your left arm for support.

7 Straddle vault over box, lengthways

This vault is a natural progression from the straddle vault over buck or box broadways, and in many ways is easier to perform as the legs do not have to be straddled as wide.

This vault should be done using a springboard. From a run up and small hurdle step on to the spring board, jump forwards and upwards to reach with outstretched arms for the far end of the box; on contact with the box, the hips must be slightly higher than the shoulders and the whole body line must be *straight*, with the shoulders completely extended.

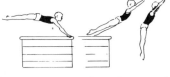

As soon as contact is made, press down hard on the box top, forcing the head and chest up so that they rise to a higher level than the hips. At the same time, straddle the legs wide, so as to complete the actual straddle vault. In flight, try to keep the body as straight as possible (with *head*

and chest held up), bending at the waist only as you bring your feet in for the landing.

In the early stages, reach as far forward as possible on the box and lower yourself slowly into a straddle sitting position. Gradually develop this until you can land on the far end of the box in straddle sit. Then, only try the full vault with a spotter present, who should help you clear the box by taking hold of your upper chest (or near upper arm) and back.

8 Rear vault

The rear vault consists of a one-quarter turn allowing the backside to pass over the top of the box, with the body bent roughly to 90°. The landing is made with the gymnast facing sideways on to the box.

From a small run and hurdle step, place both hands near the edge of the box top and jump upwards. If you intend to turn to your right, immediately release the

right hand while continuing to press strongly with the left hand and quarter turn by *looking down the length of the box*. At the same time the legs should be raised to a level above horizontal.

As soon as the quarter turn is completed, immediately replace the right hand and press down strongly while releasing the left hand to allow you to land on the other side. Do not allow any part of your body to drop until you have finished pressing away with the right hand. Then lower the feet for the landing.

A spotter can assist the gymnast by standing to his rear as he performs the vault and supporting him under his hips and shoulder.

9 Bent arm overswing

From a run up and hurdle step on to a springboard, jump forwards and upwards, placing both hands on the far edge of the box top. The jump should be powerful enough to raise the hips well above shoulder level. At the same time as the hips rise, bend the arms and allow the shoulders to move forward over your hands so that your chin drops to roughly the level of the box top. Be sure to keep your chin away from the box.

Throughout this first phase, the body will be bent slightly at the waist, so that the hips lead the feet in the first part of this vault. As the hips pass over the hands, swing the legs forward and

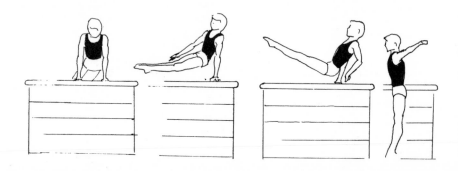

upwards while at the same time pressing strongly away with the arms. The body should be arched in flight with arms held overhead, and the head brought forward only to sight the floor in preparation for the landing.

This vault should first be done into a crash mat with a spotter present to prevent any tendency to over-rotate. Support is given under the near shoulder and lower back.

10 Kick to handstand and hold for three seconds

The handstand has been described fully earlier. The lead-up practices to being able to kick to handstand and hold it free are the same as those already mentioned.

The only points which need to be emphasised here are:

1 the handstand must be held *straight* – this position is maintained by holding the stomach in and clenching the buttocks tightly
2 balance is maintained by exerting constant pressure on the floor with the fingers.

The kick to handstand is a finely co-ordinated movement which must neither be too weak nor too strong. You must learn to feel the exact amount of pressure to be exerted on the floor so as to help you arrive in the required position. A great deal of practice every day is essential to learn this movement.

Simona Pauca, Romania, performs bent leg sissone or 'stag leap'

Stag   *Straddled*   *Splits*

Apparatus

1 Vault

The vault is the first piece of apparatus that the beginner should start on. It is an exciting and exhilarating activity suitable for all ages and easily fitted into any school or club programme.

The vault is divided into the run-up, the hurdle step, the take-off, pre-flight, strike, post-flight and landing phases. The vault consists of an aggressive approach followed by a very powerful dynamic flight-and-strike movement. During the vault, the gymnast is attempting to transfer as much power as possible from the run-up to height and flight, both of which are necessary requirements of the vault.

It is important to have a consistent run-up and to be able to take off from the 'springiest' part of the springboard every time.

Basically there are two types of vaults: horizontal vaults and vertical vaults. Horizontal vaults are where the heels rise on take-off and return back to the floor after the strike. In vertical vaults, the feet continue to rise after the strike and pass over the head to the floor.

2 Low bar

Front support
This is the most basic of positions, and it is very important to get this position absolutely right. The arms are straight, with the shoulders pressed down. The body is extended to form a straight line position if viewed from the side with the

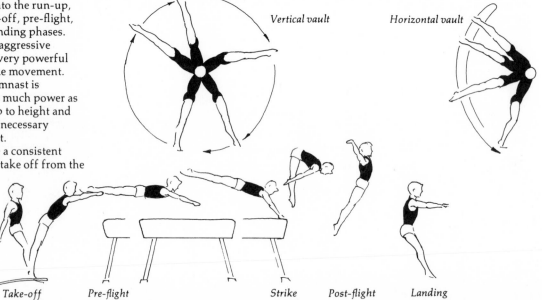

Vertical vault

Horizontal vault

Hurdle step   *Take-off*   *Pre-flight*   *Strike*   *Post-flight*   *Landing* bar running across the top of the thighs and the hands in overgrasp.

Upward circle

Standing close to the bar with bent arms and your hands in either overgrasp or undergrasp, kick one leg forwards and upwards over the bar. Keep the legs straight and very quickly bring the legs together into a piked position with the hips close to the bar and the legs over the bar. Lower the waist onto the bar by straightening the arms. The weight of the

legs will be sufficient to rotate the body to front support.

As the gymnast becomes more confident, this movement can be tried with both legs together from the floor and eventually from hang, but this will require more strength to be developed, and assistance should be given by the coach.

Underswing or shoot dismount from stand

Standing holding the bar in overgrasp, with arms straight and one foot in front of the other, swing your back leg forwards towards the bar. At the same time thrust with the foot on the ground to make your body rise. When the back leg passes the other leg, hold the legs together and allow both legs to swing to the bar. Maintain this piked position with the arms straight, the hips low and the

ankles close to the bar, as the body swings under the bar. When the body rises, quickly extend your body by driving your heels away from the bar, release the bar and shoot to stand.

This movement is particularly difficult for the beginner gymnast as it involves timing, to maximise the effects of swing and strength. In the early stages of learning this movement, the coach should support and shape the gymnast so that the performer is able to feel the correct positions throughout the movement.

Lay away

Starting from front support in overgrasp, bend the arms slightly until the waist and stomach touch the bar; the legs will swing under the bar as the shoulders move forwards. Press down with the hands on the bar and at the same time vigorously swing the legs back until the arms and body are straight. The body should rise to a position where it is parallel with the ground or higher. Throughout the lay away, your shoulders should remain forward over the bar. As the body swings down, keep yourself straight until you make contact with the bar and then allow your feet and shoulders to move forward, to arrive back in front support.

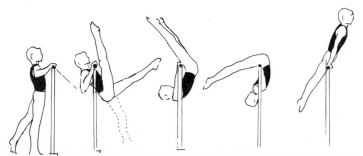

Backward circle

From the lay away, the body is swung from the shoulders back towards the bar. Tighten the muscles to maintain a slight pike and as the thighs approach the bar, lean back with the shoulders. It is important to keep the bar pressed against the thighs throughout the circle and not to let the body drop away from the bar.

To arrive in front support position without the legs going under the bar again, the gymnast must rotate his hands around the bar, slightly in advance of the body.

3 Parallel bars

Swinging in support

This is the first basic exercise on parallel bars and it must be perfected very early on to ensure that the gymnast is capable of progressing successfully to the more advanced elements.

The swing is a pendulum movement where the shoulders move forwards on the back swing and backwards on the forward swing. This movement of the shoulders is essential if the gymnast is going to maintain his support position.

The swing is developed by the chest and shoulders. The body is held straight on the forward swing until the angle at the shoulders between the body and the arms is at least a right-angle. The hips at this point can break, but the straight position should be maintained for as long as possible. As the gymnast passes through the bottom point for the back

Backward circle

swing, he starts to lean forward and swings backwards with his body straight.

It is best for the beginner gymnast to practise this in a safe situation, such as on low parallel bars with a safety mat placed under the bars.

Swinging on upper arms
Rest on the bars with your arms almost stretched out straight along the bars. The wrists should be on top of the bars with the thumb pointing downwards.

The gymnast should swing with a straight body, with the swing coming from the chest and not from just the legs.

Swinging to handstand
The idea of developing the swing to handstand should be first approached on the ground using two chalk lines to indicate the bars. The lines must be at shoulder width apart.

Having successfully mastered kicking to handstand on the two lines, without moving the hands, the skill can be transferred to two benches. Starting with the benches side by side, kick to handstand from the benches. After each successive attempt, slowly widen the benches until the gap between them is shoulder width apart. At this stage the gymnast is ready to attempt the skill on the low parallel bars.

Starting right on the end of the bars, with your back to them, try first kicking to handstand and then finally swinging to handstand. Have a coach's support in the

first stages. If you fail to make handstand then you must allow your shoulders to move forward and come down into swing. If you kick or swing too hard then you can turn out into cartwheel or drop over into the safety mat which has been placed on the end of the parallel bars.

29

4 Beam

The beam or balance beam in principle is very similar to the floor. In fact, many of the exercises practised on floor can be transferred with little difficulty, the only difference being that the beam is only 10cm wide (4in) and a greater control and precision is necessary. Many of these exercises can and should be practised on ordinary benches to gain confidence. Some of the more difficult moves should be practised with a mat over the bench.

One of the important factors to master on beam is posture; from the very beginning composure and control are essential. Start by walking briskly along the beam, keeping hips and shoulders in a straight line. Practise as many jumps as you can on beam. The most common jumps are jété and split jump.

Turns

All turns and pivots should be performed on the toes. As you turn, rise up onto the toes with the arms above the head. The

most basic turn is a turn on two feet. Standing one leg in front of the other, extend the legs and ankles until on your toes. Swing your arm up and back but slightly to one side, push through the front leg and half turn, taking the weight evenly between both feet.

Half spin on one foot

Stepping forward onto the extended ankle, raise your arms above your head to initiate the turn. Hold your head up and, having completed the turn, very quickly fix your gaze to regain your balance. You can turn either inwards or outwards. The inward turn is normally easier as both feet stay on the beam longer.

Mounts on beam

Squat-on: Standing facing the beam with your hands shoulder width apart, place your hands on the beam and jump off both feet. Try to raise your hips above your shoulders and press down with your

arms. As your hips rise above your shoulders, bend your legs and squat onto the beam. Transfer your weight from your hands to your feet and stand up on the balls of your feet.

Straddle mount from front support: Place your hands on the beam with your fingers just over the far edge and jump to front support. Swing one leg sideways, simultaneously transferring your weight to the opposite arm. As your leg rises above the height of the beam, swing your leg forward (and momentarily raise your free hand from the beam), allowing your leg to swing to the front. On replacing your hand, quarter turn your body to face your supporting hand and sit astride the beam. Place both hands in front of you on the beam. Press down, allow your

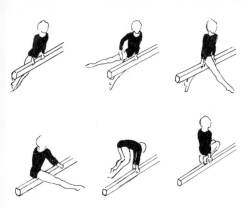

shoulders to move forward and swing your legs back to squat on the beam.

Forward roll on beam

This movement should first be practised on benches. This is essentially the same as the forward roll on floor as described earlier, except that the hands will be placed much closer together to grip the beam. The gymnast's thumb should be across the beam with the hand spread out down the sides of the beam. This will result in the elbows being kept close to the head throughout the first stage of the roll. The roll should be fairly fast but controlled with the back kept well rounded. The gymnast can finish the roll as on floor in crouch but, to aid balance, should have one foot slightly in front of the other, reaching well forward with the arms to allow him to obtain weight over the feet to stand.

The forward roll can also be performed as a mount on the end of the beam, using a springboard to obtain the necessary lift for the gymnast to be able to tuck the head in.

Cartwheel

This movement should first be performed on a chalked line on the floor, and when the technique has been fully mastered with no twisting of the body then the skill can be transferred to a bench and then finally to the beam.

The cartwheel is very similar to the one described on floor except that on beam, the gymnast normally performs a quarter turn inwards as the feet come down to the beam to allow him to see where his feet have to be placed and to facilitate a firmer, more controlled landing.

The cartwheel is performed as on floor but is not so long, as the quarter turn inwards shortens the second phase of the cartwheel owing to the first leg landing closer to the hands. The cartwheel can be performed as a dismount.

Normally the feet are brought together and a strong thrust from the beam is executed to give the dismount flight. The gymnast lands with the feet together.

Handstand

The handstand on beam can be performed with legs straight, split, or one leg straight and one leg bent (stag). The technique is the same as on floor except that the thumbs are placed along the beam and the fingers down the side. As

described earlier, the back is kept straight and the arms are raised above the head. In the early stages this can be practised on a bench. The coach should assist you until confidence is gained and you are aware of what to do should you kick too hard.

extent of your suppleness. Continue lifting your leg as you lower your chest, keeping your head up. This will hollow your back. Your arms can either be forward or to the side but they should follow the hollow line that the raised leg and body make.

Arabesque

Start by standing on one leg with the other leg stretched behind you with the top of your toe resting on the beam. Slowly raise the leg upwards behind you, keeping your back straight, having fixed your gaze on some point in front of you. Continue to raise your leg to the full

5 Advanced floor agilities

Back somersault

There are two different ways of approaching the back somersault. One way is as an individual movement, the other more general way is by performing the movement immediately from a round-off back flip.

Considering the movement as performed on its own, start from standing and slightly bend the knees, making sure not to lean forward. The arms are swung forwards and upwards, keeping them straight, to a point just above the head. Simultaneously, the legs thrust forcefully on the ground. The gymnast should think mainly of thrusting and drawing his hips up over his head. Having left the floor, the gymnast tucks to increase his speed of rotation. When the gymnast sees the floor, he should open out to control the landing.

Forward somersault

The movement is best learned from a raised platform (such as a box top) onto a safety mat. In the early stages of learning, the coach should aid the movement by standing to the gymnast's side with one hand placed on his lower back. The coach aids the gymnast by lifting him with the hand placed on his back and rotating him with the hand placed just below the backside.

Forward somersault

The approach consists of a short run and a hurdle step from one foot to two. As the feet contact the floor, the body rocks forwards and upwards (around the feet as a pivot) until the take-off. On take-off, the gymnast should be leaning slightly backwards as both feet thrust from the floor. It is important that the gymnast does not lean forwards. The gymnast therefore is aiming to keep his body upright during the take-off. One important factor in obtaining height in the somersault is to get the head and chest up. The arms aid the movement by being thrown forcefully upwards, either forwards or backwards, at the instant of take-off and whilst the feet are still in contact with the ground. It is the co-ordinated action of arm throw and leg-hip extension which gives the gymnast good height.

Once in flight, the gymnast should fold into a tight tuck position to aid the rotation of the somersault. When using the back armlift action, the gymnast generally grasps his legs behind his thighs, while in the forward armlift action it is usual to grasp the legs just below the knee. Just before landing, 'open out' by sharply extending the legs and hips.

The coach should assist the gymnast by taking hold of the stomach at take-off and allowing the gymnast to rotate around the coach's arm. In this way the coach can not only aid the gymnast throughout the movement but also time the gymnast 'out' of the somersault for a good landing.

Another useful aid in helping the gymnast to obtain lift in the somersault is shown below:

33

The gymnast rolls over the platform, made up of safety mats, which starts low but is gradually raised.

Always use extra mats when performing somersaults and where possible use safety mats in the early stages of learning.

Backward walk-over
Starting from standing, stretch your arms above your head. Raise one leg forward with the toe pointed sufficiently to a point where the toe is lightly touching the floor; the weight should be fully on the other leg. Extend the shoulders by pressing the arms back behind the ears and head. Continue to press the arms backwards and allow the back to bend slowly and progressively from the shoulders down to the lower back, until the hands are lowered onto the floor.

Throughout the movement make sure that the hips remain square and do not twist. Simultaneously, as the back is bending, the forward leg is lifting over the head through splits position and then down to the floor. Push from the floor with your hands, keeping the back straight and pass through arabesque position to stand. Throughout the movement the arms remain stretched above your head and by your ears.

6 Advanced apparatus

The upstart: low bar
This movement is very similar in action to the upstart on the other pieces of apparatus and basically allows the gymnast to move from a position of hang into one of support.

The gymnast starts by swinging on the hands in overgrasp with legs stretched out in front (float). When his body reaches the extent of the forward swing in an extended position, with the shoulders extended by pressing back with the hands, he bends rapidly at the waist bringing the feet close to the bar. The body then swings back under the bar and the hips are extended while pressing downwards with straight arms. The bar moves along the legs to the thighs as the body continues to rotate up into front support. The hands are moved around the bar in advance of the body to allow for a strong support position to be achieved.

There are many different positions and grasps. The most important of these grasps are the overgrasp and the undergrasp. The grasp of the bar can vary in many different ways depending on the movement the gymnast is attempting. It is important to note that the fingers are always trailing the movement around the bar.

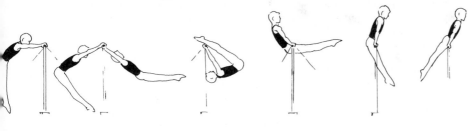

The upstart: parallel bars

Swing forward in hang maintaining complete extension in the shoulders, while the feet glide forward just above the floor. As the gymnast reaches full extension, he quickly bends at the hip and brings his feet to his hands. He swings back in this position bringing the legs closer to the face; as the shoulders begin to rise, the hips are extended and a strong downward push is performed to raise the body up to front support.

The upward thrust is therefore created during the second half of the backward pendulum swing.

Li Ning, China, does a 'Diamidov' – a swinging full turn to handstand

Body preparation and conditioning

Preparation of the body is probably the first and most important aspect to be considered in the training of a young gymnast. A good level of physical condition is essential for the later learning of more advanced movements and the development of correct techniques. Without good technique (which should be tackled early on in the gymnast's career), the gymnast will find his progress severely limited. For example, the development of double leg circles on the pommel horse requires a minimum level of physical condition in order to hold the body in an extended fashion away from the horse.

The well-prepared gymnast scores highly in terms of both strength and endurance. Strength is the amount of force that can be exerted in one maximum contraction, and both men's and women's gymnastics require varied types of strength for maximum execution. The gymnast must be strong enough to hold his body in support and in hang while performing various gymnastic movements, and must also be able to hold his body in a straight position for those movements that require it. These movements may be either explosive, slow or stationary in nature.

Endurance, on the other hand, is the ability to continue an activity over an extended period of time. Muscular strength and endurance cannot be developed independently as the two are related. Maximum strength is developed with few repetitions and high resistance (weight), while endurance is developed with many repetitions and low resistance. For example, in pushing to handstands, maximum strength can be developed by adding extra resistance such as a weight belt, while maximum endurance is enhanced by doing as many repetitions as possible in a single set.

Below are shown some general exercises covering the main body parts. As his overall level of physcial condition improves, the gymnast should then spend more time on specific exercises which are more relevant to gymnastic performance. Such exercises should be performed directly on the apparatus concerned.

Arm and shoulder
1 Push ups . . . raising level of legs to . . .
2 Handstand push ups
3 Chins
4 Shoulder shrugging in handstand (against wall)

Abdominals
1 Sit ups
2 V sits
3 In hang, raise legs to touch bar

Back
1 Lying on stomach, raise chest and legs (many repetitions done fast, or with static hold on each repetition)
2 Lying on stomach, on end of box top (with partner sitting on legs), raise chest

Legs
1 Standing long jumps down length of mats
2 Run (or jump) up and down flight of stairs
3 Use of leg machines in weight room (avoid deep knee bends)
4 General running for endurance

Warm-up

The warm-up is a most essential part of any training programme and the gymnast should quickly get into the habit of warming up at the beginning of every gymnastic session. The purpose of warming up is to prepare the gymnast's body for the more strenuous work which follows. It can also have a positive effect on the gymnast's mind in that he often feels better as a result of it.

A good active warm-up is also a helpful aid in the prevention of injuries, as any increase in muscle temperature helps minimise the risk of injury.

The warm-up generally consists of jogging and running to raise the overall body temperature, which is then closely followed by stretching and limbering exercises. Young gymnasts should at all costs avoid walking into the gymnasium and then dropping immediately into splits: torn hamstrings can be very painful and take a long time to heal.

Typical warm-up
Always wear plenty of clothing including a track suit and sweat suit if available. Then start by generally jogging, running and skipping around the gymnasium until the body is nice and warm. Exercises which use the majority of the gymnast's muscles can be included, such as arm and leg swinging, and trunk circling. Games such as tig, chain, leap-frog and catch are also very useful motivators.

Once in a warm state the gymnast should progress to more specific (suppling) exercises for all the major joints, i.e. wrists, elbows, shoulders, neck, back, hips, knees and ankles. The latter are dealt with in greater detail in the next section.

Suppling

Suppling is the method by which flexibility or range of movement is increased. Suppling is essential, not only because it allows the correct body positions to be developed, but also because maximum range of movement can minimise injuries when muscles are accidentally overstretched. Even a handstand can be difficult for the gymnast with stiff shoulders.

All body parts must be considered under this aspect of the training programme.

Essential suppling exercises

Spine
1 Bend forwards, backwards and
   sideways (while standing)

2 Forward bend with chest on thighs (sitting)

3 Shoulder balance with feet touching the floor

4 Bridge

Hips and legs

1 Leg swinging, forward, backward and sideways

2 Straddle sit with chest on the floor

3 Splits, forward and sideways

4 Sit on heels; place hands on ankles and arch back

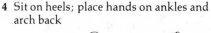

Shoulders

1 Arm swinging, forward, backward and in a circular fashion

2 Shoulder extension (kneeling on floor) or against wall bars

3 Shoulder flexion (sitting on floor) or against wall bars

4 Holding stick, dislocate and inlocate at shoulder joints

Wrists

1 Press palms flat on floor with fingers pointing forward, backward and sideways

2 Wrist circling with fingers intertwined

Knees

1 Sit back on heels – then move feet apart and lie with back flat on the floor

Ankles

1 Lean towards wall with feet flat on the floor

2 Sit on heels and lift knees off floor

Safety

Safety is probably the most important factor in any gymnastic environment. Injuries incurred through negligence can have a negative effect on the gymnast which may result in him giving up gymnastics altogether. To ensure a completely safe gymnastic environment, two aspects need to be considered: layout of equipment, and performance and the learning of new movements.

Layout of equipment

1 The first duty of the coach is to check the apparatus before use. Make sure it is firmly anchored to the ground, with adjustments and cables being sufficiently tightened to minimise excessive movement.
2 The apparatus should be well spaced so that the dismount areas from each piece of equipment do not interfere with one another. Allow for the unexpected.
3 If a foam pit is not available, then sufficient mats must be arranged, beneath and around the apparatus. Use large foam rubber mattresses to ensure further safety.
4 There should be no cracks or spaces left between mats – press them well together.

Performance and the learning of new movements

1 *Training should only take place in the presence of a qualified coach, who should be in attendance at all times.*
2 Warm up thoroughly before starting serious training, preferably in a well-heated gymnasium.
3 When in the process of learning new movements or any movement which involves a degree of risk, the gymnast should only attempt this in the presence of a coach. The gymnast's safety should be ensured at all times, by the use of foam pits or safety mattresses, and the learning process should be sufficiently progressive, so that the gymnast is not taxed too far beyond his present level of ability.

   The coach should also be capable of spotting (giving physical assistance) to the gymnast when necessary.

Index

Andrew Morris, Great Britain, →
straddled planché on parallel bars